Geri Halliwell

Julia Holt

Published in association with The Basic Skills Agency

Hodder & Stoughton

A MEMBER OF THE HODDER HEADLINE GROUP

Acknowledgements
Cover: Tapham Picturepaint

Photos: pp. iv, 24 © All Action, pp. 3, 12, 20 © Retna, p. 6 © Topham, p. 27 Alpha.

Every effort has been made to trace copyright holders of material rproduced in this book. Any rights not acknowledged will be acknowledged in subsequent printings if notice is given to the publisher.

Orders; please contact Bookpoint Ltd, 39 Milton Park, Abingdon, Oxon OX14 4TD. Telephone (44) 01235 400414, Fax: (44) 01235 400454. Lines are oprn from 9.00–6.00, Monday to Saturday, with a 24 hour message answering service.
Emails address: orders©bookpoint.co.uk

British Library Cataloguing in Publication Data
A catalogue record for this title is available from the British Library

ISBN 0 340 80088 7

First published 2001
Impression number   10 9 8 7 6 5 4 3 2 1
Year   2007 2006 2005 2004 2003 2002 2001

Copyright © Julia Holt

Typeset by SX Composing DTP, Rayleigh, Essex
Printed in Great Britain for Hodder & Stoughton Educational, a division of Hodder Headline Plc, 338 Euston Road, London NW1 3BH by Redwood Books, Trowbridge, Wiltshire

Contents

Geri Halliwell was a member of the biggest girl band in the world – the Spice Girls. Why did she leave?

1 Introduction

In May 1998
a young woman
left the biggest girl band in the world.
She always wanted to be famous
and she was.
But she still walked away
from the Spice Girls.

She didn't know what to do
or if her fans would forget her.
Her name is Geri Halliwell.
She is still famous.
Her fans did not forget her.

2 Geri's Early Life

Geri was born on 6 August 1972,
in Watford.
She was the third child in the family.
Her brother Max had Dad's blond hair.
Her sister Natalie had Mum's dark hair.
Geri had red hair.
There were two other children,
Karen and Paul,
from their Dad's first marriage.

The family lived
in a small pebble-dashed house
in Watford.
Their Spanish mum, Ana-Maria,
went to work as a cleaner at 6am.
So Geri got herself ready for school.

From the start
Geri wanted to be famous.
She pretended to be on TV
and she sang along to the radio.
She wanted to live in a castle
when she grew up.

Geri always wanted to be famous even when she was young.

In the summer holidays
the family went to Spain
to see their grandmother.
But Dad always stayed at home.
He was a dreamer and didn't work much.
Geri's parents were often arguing.

One day, when Geri was small,
all three children were sent away.
Geri went to stay with her stepsister Karen.
When she came back, Dad had moved out.

As the three children grew up
they were very close.
Geri followed Natalie everywhere.
Aged 11, Geri went to Watford Grammar School.
She was a small, clumsy girl
with braces on her teeth.
But her talent for singing helped her to fit in.

Every week Geri went to see her Dad.
He gave her money to clean his flat.
She was often in trouble with her Mum.
But her Dad helped her to dream
of being famous.

3 Geri's Teenage Years

Geri wanted to be famous
like George Michael.
He was her hero
But the 14-year-old girl
only had £1.50 a week pocket money.
She needed a Saturday job.

Geri delivered newspapers,
sold ice-cream, and fish and chips.
Then she got a job in Next clothes shop.
She spent all her money
on clothes from the market.
She wanted to look like
the girls on *Top of the Pops*.

George Michael was Geri's hero. Later he became her friend.

4 What Next?

In the Summer of 1988
Geri chose to leave school.
Big brother Max went to university
and big sister Natalie went to college.
Geri didn't know what to do
so she followed Natalie to college
to study travel.

But Geri didn't want to *study* travel,
she wanted to *do* it.
That year she went on holiday
with two girl friends
and had a great time.

The next year
Geri got a job at the Hilton Hotel.
Her mum was proud of her.
But Geri missed her Friday nights out,
so she left the job.
Geri and her Mum argued
so she left home to live in Dad's flat.

Geri's next project was learning to drive.
One night, after two driving lessons,
she took her Dad's car
and drove into London.
When she got home
the police were waiting for her.

Geri's Dad threw her out
and she went to live
with her stepsister Karen.

In the Summer of 1989
there were rave parties all over England.
Thousands of young people
danced all night
in odd places, like farmers' fields.
Geri loved going to raves.
One night, after a rave,
she had a big party at Karen's house.
Karen threw her out.

Dad didn't want her back.
She was unemployed.
She danced all night and slept all day.
Geri ended up living in a squat.

5 Geri's Illnesses

Geri took part-time jobs
posing for photos and dancing in nightclubs.
Now she had the money
to do up the squat and buy a bike.
She rode round Watford
in a silver swimsuit
and white hot pants!

Two months later a letter came
telling her to get out of the squat.
Geri had to sleep in a car.
She didn't want to go home.

By Christmas of 1990
she had moved into a bedsit.
She went home for Christmas dinner.
At home she looked in a mirror
and saw her black eyes and thin face.
Geri had to change her life.

She enrolled in an A level Drama class.
She studied plays and acting.
But one day
she was putting on her bra
when she found a lump in her breast.
Geri and her Mum went to the hospital.
The lump was taken out
and Geri was OK
but very, very scared.

In March 1991
Geri's life did change.
She got a job dancing
in Majorca.
She was paid £20 a night.
She danced in a cage
from 12am to 5am.

Majorca gave Geri the chance
to get fit and well.
She ate good food
and swam every day.
Mum and her new boyfriend, Steve,
came out to see her.

Back in London
Geri posed for photos again.
She was Miss April in a calendar
and she was paid £400 for it.
For some of the photos
she was in the nude.
But her career as a model
didn't take off.
All that swimming in Majorca
had given her muscles.
She thought the muscles made her look big.

Geri felt that she was fat
so she made herself throw up.
It became a very bad habit.
She had bulimia.

6 Working Abroad

In 1992 Geri was modelling again,
in Greece and Spain.
But she wasn't happy.
She was living in dirty flats
and she was being treated badly.
So she came home.
She was finished with modelling.

Back in London
Geri tried to get jobs in TV.
Her Dad went with her to auditions
but she had no success.
Then one day
she went to audition
as a TV game show hostess.

The job was in Turkey
and Geri was chosen.
She went to Istanbul for three weeks
and she did three shows a day.
Geri didn't speak Turkish
so she had to pretend that she did.
She became very popular in Turkey.
But after three weeks
she had to come back
to look for her big break in England.

Geri had to work hard to get where she is today.

Back in London again
Geri set herself up as a fitness trainer.
She still went to many, many auditions.
By the time she was 21 years old
she had a thick file of letters,
all turning her down.

In 1993 she was back in Istanbul
doing the game show again.
At least they wanted her.
She spent weekdays in London
and weekends in Istanbul.

One weekday the phone rang.
It was Max.
He told her that their Dad was dead.
Geri had lost her No. 1 fan.
She stopped eating
and went down to six stones.
Everyone tried to get her to eat
But she hardly ever did.
That year Christmas was very sad.

In 1994 Geri pulled herself together.
She paid £300 to record two songs.
They weren't very good
but she was hopeful.

Then in May,
she spotted an advert
that she'd stuck on her mirror months before,
it said:

> **RU 18-23**
> with the ability to
> sing/dance?

She was very late
but she phoned anyway.
Geri just made the final audition.
They were looking for an all-girl band.
They were down to the last 12.
Geri was chosen
and the rest is history.

7 Starting Out with the Spice Girls

The five chosen girls lived together
in a rented house.
They all wanted to be rich and famous.
They all worked very hard.
Geri was still very thin
and she wasn't eating much
but Mel B helped her.
They became firm friends.

Towards the end of 1994
the band had a name 'Spice'
and a few songs.
Geri turned into Ginger Spice
and Girl Power was born.

In July 1995
they signed up with Virgin Records.
They were each paid £10,000.
But they didn't make a record
for another year.

Geri was happy to be part of a team.
The Spice Girls went to the USA,
they went on holiday together
and they spent hours recording songs.

It took quite a long time for the Spice Girls to become famous.

By February 1996,
Geri was living with the two Mels.
She got her first sports car.
It was bright red.
She gave each Spice Girl
a gold ring
with SPICE written on the inside.

In April they made the video
for their single, 'Wannabee'.
They filmed the video
in a big, empty building.
Geri's outfit cost her £20
from the market.
The video cost £130,000 to make.

'Wannabee' was a big success
when it came out in July.
They were in Japan
when it went to No.1
From then on the Spice Girls
were swept away by fame.

8 Hitting the Big Time

Life for Geri and the girls
became very hectic.
They were all very tired.
Geri's bulimia came back.
Some of her nude photos
were in the papers.
Old boyfriends sold stories
to the papers.
But the fans loved the Spice Girls.
Their first album went to No. 1

Geri soon found out
how important her family and friends were.
She took her best friend
on holiday at the end of 1996.
It was just what she needed.
After the two-week holiday
it was back to work.

In 1997 there was Comic Relief,
the Brit Awards, touring,
a new album and *Spice World, The Movie.*
Geri also met her hero, George Michael.
They became friends.

In September 1997
the girls set off on a long tour.
The first stop was Istanbul.
Three years before that Geri had been
a game show hostess there.
Now she was a superstar.

But there was no time
for the girls to rest.
Geri was unhappy.
Her bulimia was getting worse.
She asked for time off
but was told 'No'.

Geri was thinking of leaving the group.
But the girls sacked their manager
and chose to stick together.
They kept the tour going.
They were No. 1 in Christmas 1997,
for the second year running.

Geri started to change from Ginger Spice, back to Geri.

The tour rolled on in 1998.
The girls went to Australia,
the USA and Ireland.
Geri told the girls
that she wanted to leave
at the end of the tour in September.
They were very hurt.
They started planning
without Geri.
She started to change
from Ginger Spice, back to Geri.
She was growing up.

Geri started to wear less make-up
and her hair changed to blonde.
On the 27 May 1998
she couldn't wait any longer.
She left the band.

9 Geri's New Life

Geri felt good
but where could she go
to keep away from the papers?
She went to Paris
with her brother Max.
Every paper in the world
was looking for her.

George Michael
asked her to come and stay with him.
George and his partner Kenny
took her to LA with them.

In LA Geri got all her energy back.
She liked looking after herself,
making her own choices.
But she didn't know
if she could make it alone.

Geri threw herself into charity work.
She sold all her Spice Girls clothes
and her bright red sports car.
Her home-made Union Jack dress
sold for £36,000.
The money went to charity.
Then she started
to write a book about herself.
It was called *If Only*.
The profits from the book
went to a breast cancer charity.

In September 1998
she flew back to England.
Geri had plans for her new home.
It was an old monastery
and it needed doing up.
She also had plans
for a solo album.

Geri spends a lot of time doing charity work for charities like Breast Cancer Awareness.

Then one day a letter came
from the United Nations.
They wanted Geri
to be a Goodwill Ambassador.
They wanted her to tell the world
about family planning.
She was so excited
and her Mum was very proud of her.

She also went to Uganda
for Comic Relief.
She made a film in Uganda
about people learning to read and write.
Comic Relief were helping the people there.

Geri also found time
to sing 'Happy Birthday' to Prince Charles.
George and Kenny went with her.
She was making her comeback.

Geri's book came out in 1999
and so did her solo album.
It was called *Schizophonic*.
For the next year
she had hit after hit
with singles from *Schizophonic*.

March 2000 was a big month
for Geri.
Her single 'Bag It Up'
was racing up the charts.
Then she stole the show
at the Brit Awards.
She came on to the stage
from a pair of blow up legs.
That one song
cost £100,000 to put on the stage.
It was a big success.

Geri's solo career is a huge success.

In May, Geri's Mum and Steve
got married.
She sang for them
and all her friends were there.

Her next project is a film.
It's called *Therapy*.
Geri stars as a young woman
who falls in love with her therapist.
She is writing songs for the film.
So the film and her next album
will be linked together.

Geri is also going to Kosovo
with Robbie Williams.
They will sing for the people there.

Geri's Dad told her
never to say 'if only'
and she hasn't.
She has always followed her dreams.